2 x 7/15 LT 6/15

WITHDRAWN

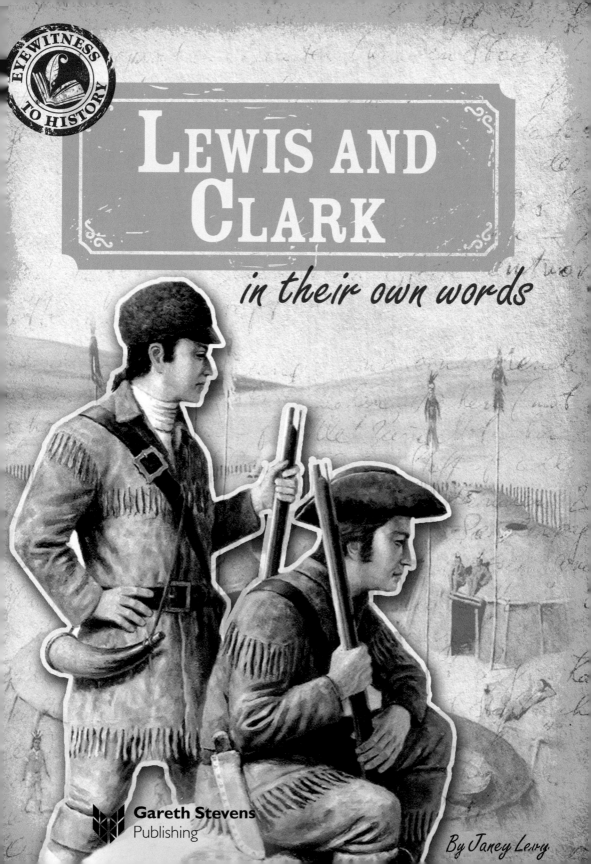

EYEWITNESS TO HISTORY

LEWIS AND CLARK

in their own words

Gareth Stevens
Publishing

By Janey Levy

Please visit our website, www.garethstevens.com. For a free color catalog of all our high-quality books, call toll free 1-800-542-2595 or fax 1-877-542-2596.

Library of Congress Cataloging-in-Publication Data

Levy, Janey.
Lewis and Clark in their own words / by Janey Levy.
   p. cm. — (Eyewitness to history)
Includes index.
ISBN 978-1-4339-9930-7 (pbk.)
ISBN 978-1-4339-9931-4 (6-pack)
ISBN 978-1-4339-9929-1 (library binding)
1. West (U.S.) — Discovery and exploration — Juvenile literature. 2. Lewis, Meriwether, — 1774-1809 — Juvenile literature. 3. Clark, William, — 1770-1838 — Juvenile literature. I. Levy, Janey. II. Title.
F592.7 L48 2014
917.804—dc23

First Edition

Published in 2014 by
Gareth Stevens Publishing
111 East 14th Street, Suite 349
New York, NY 10003

Copyright © 2014 Gareth Stevens Publishing

Designer: Katelyn E. Reynolds
Editor: Therese Shea

Photo credits: Cover, p. 1 USCapitol/Wikipedia.com; cover, p. 1 (logo quill icon) Seamartini Graphics Media/Shutterstock.com; cover, p. 1 (logo stamp) YasnaTen/Shutterstock.com; cover, p. 1 (color grunge frame) DmitryPrudnichenko/Shutterstock.com; cover, pp. 1–32 (paper background) Nella/Shutterstock.com; cover, pp. 1–32 (decorative elements) Ozerina Anna/Shutterstock.com; pp. 1–32 (wood texture) Reinhold Leitner/Shutterstock.com; pp. 1–32 (open book background) Elena Schweitzer/Shutterstock.com; pp. 1–32 (bookmark) Robert Adrian Hillman/Shutterstock.com; pp. 4, 8–9, 13, 24–25 MPI/Getty Images; p. 5 (both signatures) McSush/Wikipedia.com; p. 7 John Elk/Lonely Planet Images/Getty Images; pp. 10–11 Prisma/UIG/Getty Images; p. 15 Dorling Kindersley RF/Thinkstock.com; p. 17 DEA/G. SIOEN/De Agostini/Getty Images; pp. 18–19 SuperStock/Getty Images; pp. 20–21 L.A. Nature Graphics/Shutterstock.com; p. 23 B. Anthony Stewart/National Geographic/Getty Images; p. 27 Kean Collection/Archive Photos/Getty Images; pp. 28–29 (map) Uwe Dedering/Wikipedia.com.

Printed in the United States of America

CPSIA compliance information: Batch #CW14GS: For further information contact Gareth Stevens, New York, New York at 1-800-542-2595.

CONTENTS

*Words in the glossary appear in **bold** type the first time they are used in the text.*

The TERRITORY Ahead

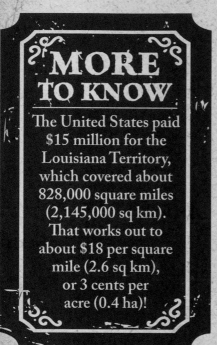
A single event in 1803 changed the United States forever. The country's western edge had been the Mississippi River ever since the United States became independent in 1783. But with the purchase of the Louisiana Territory from France, the country suddenly doubled in size.

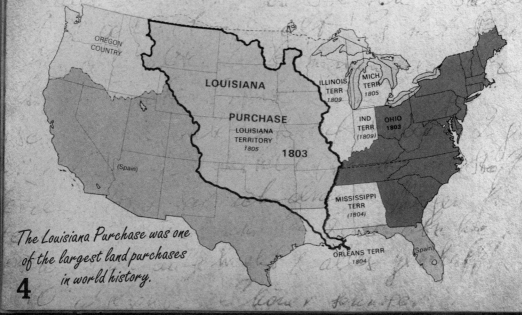

The Louisiana Purchase was one of the largest land purchases in world history.

The Louisiana Territory stretched from the Mississippi River to the Rocky Mountains, and from the Gulf of Mexico to Canada. Maps of the time showed large empty spaces there because mapmakers knew little about the region. President Thomas Jefferson charged Meriwether Lewis with leading an expedition to explore the new territory. Lewis asked William Clark to lead with him. Jefferson instructed the men to learn all they could about the land and the animals, plants, and native people who lived there.

Meriwether Lewis's actual signature:

Meriwether Lewis

William Clark's actual signature:

William Clark

JEFFERSON'S SECRET LETTER TO CONGRESS

Even before the Louisiana Territory was purchased, Jefferson secretly asked Congress to fund an expedition. He explained the expedition would improve knowledge about the Indians of the region and promote trade with them, adding, *"that it should incidentally advance the geographical knowledge of our own continent, cannot be but an additional gratification."* His language may sound strange to us, but he simply meant that the fact the expedition would also improve knowledge of the geography was an additional benefit.

PREPARATIONS

Preparing for an expedition across an immense, uncharted territory was no easy task. Lewis and Clark studied mapmaking, medicine, plant life, and other areas of science that might be helpful on their journey. They also had to assemble a team, have a boat built, and buy supplies and equipment. Here are items from the supply list, as Lewis wrote them:

THE FIRST BLACK MAN TO CROSS THE CONTINENT

The expedition included Clark's slave, York. Clark and York were about the same age and had grown up together. York was an equal member of the expedition, taking part in all the activities and tasks. When Clark and three others were caught in a storm, a worried York risked his life to search for them. Clark recorded that when they reached safety, *"I found my servent in serch [search] of us greatly agitated, for our wellfar [welfare]."*

Scientific Instruments:
3 Thermometers, 1 Cheap portable Microscope, 1 Pocket Compass, Books, Maps, Charts

Camp Equipage:
6 Copper kettles, 3 Coils of rope, 1 Iron Mill for Grinding Corn, 4 Tin blowing Trumpets, 24 Iron Spoons, 24 Pint Tin Cups (without handles)

Provisions:
150 lbs. Portable Soup

Indian Presents:
5 lbs. White Glass Beads mostly small, 12 Red Silk Hanckerchiefs [handkerchiefs], 144 Small cheap looking Glasses, 144 Small cheap Scizors [scissors], 15 Sheets of Copper, 20 Sheets of Tin

MORE TO KNOW

Thomas Jefferson created secret codes to be used in communications between himself and Lewis.

This statue shows Lewis and Clark along with York and Lewis's dog, Seaman. Lewis purchased the Newfoundland dog before the expedition, and Seaman made the entire journey with them.

The
EXPEDITION
Begins

MORE TO KNOW

People in the early 1800s often spelled words differently than we do today, but you can usually figure out a word by sounding it out. They also didn't follow the same rules for capitalization and punctuation that we do.

We know a great deal about day-to-day life as well as major events on the expedition because Lewis and Clark both kept journals. In fact, Clark recorded the gloomy weather in which they set out from St. Louis, Missouri, on

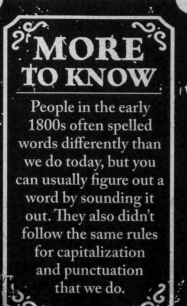

Meriwether Lewis and William Clark met with Native Americans of the Missouri and Oto tribes at Council Bluffs, Iowa, on August 3, 1804.

May 14, 1804: *"I Set out at 4 oClock P.M. . . . and proceeded on under a jentle brease [gentle breeze] up the Missourie [Missouri River] . . . a heavy rain this after-noon."*

In early August, the **Corps** of Discovery—as the group was called—had its first official encounter with Native Americans. The explorers exchanged gifts with Oto and Missouri Indians. Clark wrote, *"Sent them Some rosted [roasted] meat, Pork flour & meal, in return they sent us Water millions [watermelons]."*

THE GREAT PLAINS

When they reached South Dakota, Lewis was struck by the beauty of the **plains** and the abundance of wildlife. He wrote, *"this senery [scenery] already rich pleasing and beatiful [beautiful] was still farther hightened by immence [immense] herds of Buffaloe, deer Elk and **Antelopes** which we saw in every direction feeding on the hills and plains. I do not think I exagerate when I estimate the number of Buffaloe . . . to amount to 3000."*

THE SAD STORY OF THE OMAHA INDIANS

In mid-August, the expedition encountered the Omaha Indians. Like many other tribes, they had been nearly wiped out by smallpox, a terrible disease brought to North America by colonists. Clark recorded: *"I am told when this fatal **malady** was among them they Carried their franzey [frenzy] to verry extroordinary length, not only of burning their Village, but they put their wives & children to Death with a view of their all going together to some better Countrey."*

In late August 1804, the expedition encountered the Yankton Sioux Indians in South Dakota. The tribe's buffalo-skin **tepees** and orderly villages impressed Clark, who wrote, *"the Scioues [Sioux's] Camps are handsom of a Conic form Covered with Buffalow Roabs [robes] Painted different colours and all compact & handsomly arranged."*

Clark noted the Sioux themselves were a strong, attractive people. He was particularly struck by the warriors, with their war paint, porcupine **quills**, and feathers.

This picture of a Sioux village near Fort Laramie, Wyoming, clearly shows their tepees and gives an idea of their clothing and daily life.

He recorded their appearance in some detail:

"The Souex [Sioux] is a Stout bold looking people, & well made . . . the Warriers [warriors] are Verry much deckerated [decorated] with Paint Porcupine quils & feathers, large leagins [leggings] and mockersons [moccasins], all with buffalow roabs [robes] of Different Colours."

MORE TO KNOW

In early September, the expedition saw unfamiliar animals on a hillside. Clark identified them as goats. But the animals weren't goats—they were antelopes!

WINTER

at Fort Mandan

MORE TO KNOW

The Mandan and Hidatsa villages were home to about 4,500 people. That's more than the population of Washington, DC, at the time!

In late October 1804, the expedition reached Mandan and Hidatsa Indian villages in North Dakota. They needed sturdy shelter for the coming winter, so Lewis and Clark chose a nearby spot to build a fort. By late December, Fort Mandan was completed.

Lewis and Clark continued preparations for the journey during the winter. To help them communicate with Indians farther west, they hired an interpreter with a young Shoshone Indian wife. Toussaint Charbonneau was a French-Canadian trapper living among the Hidatsa. His wife was Sacagawea.

It was a long, hard winter. By mid-February 1805, the expedition had run out of meat. They hunted when possible, but as Lewis complained, the wolves often ate what the hunters killed. Finally, in early April, the expedition could set out again.

*This drawing of Sacagawea is from 1810.
However, no one really knows what she looked like.*

SO COLD

The extreme cold of winter on the northern plains shocked the explorers. Clark made numerous entries recording the temperature. On December 8, 1804, he wrote, *"the Thermometer Stood at 12 d [degrees] below 0 which is 42 d below the freesing [freezing] point."* Soon, it was even colder. It was 21 degrees below zero on December 11 and 38 degrees below zero on December 12. On December 17, Clark recorded: *"45 d. below 0."*

From FORT MANDAN
to the Great Falls

URSUS ARCTOS HORRIBILIS

The expedition provided the first scientific description of the grizzly bear, whose Latin name is *Ursus arctos horribilis*. Native Americans had told the explorers about grizzlies, but the expedition didn't encounter one until late April 1805. Lewis recorded his experience: *"it is a much more furious and formidable anamal, and will frequently pursue the hunter when wounded. it is asstonishing to see the wounds they will bear before they can be put to death. the Indians may well fear this anamal."*

Lewis and Clark sent the largest boat and about 12 men back down the Missouri River, along with maps, reports, Indian objects, and boxes of scientific specimens for President Jefferson. The permanent party—Lewis, Clark, York, Charbonneau, Sacagawea, Sacagawea's baby boy, 27 soldiers, and the dog Seaman—headed west. Lewis recorded his excitement and that of the whole party: *"I could but esteem this moment of my departure as among the most happy of my life. The party are in excellent health and sperits [spirits] ... and anxious to proceed."*

As the expedition journeyed west, the explorers were astonished by the abundance of wildlife—elks,

14

antelopes, and buffalo herds numbering 10,000. They were also astonished by how tame the animals seemed, not trying to flee from them.

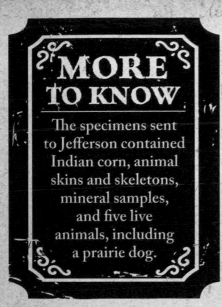

This is an artist's idea of the Lewis and Clark expedition having an encounter with some grizzly bears.

When Lewis saw the Rocky Mountains for the first time in late May 1805, he was both thrilled and sober: *"when I reflected on the difficulties which this snowey barrier would most probably throw in my way to the Pacific, and the sufferings and hardships of myself and party in thim [them], it in some measure counterballanced the joy I had felt."*

MORE TO KNOW

Lewis and Clark had expected it to take about half a day to get around the Great Falls. Because of bad weather and other obstacles, it took nearly a month!

On June 2, the expedition reached a fork in the Missouri River and had to choose one. Lewis scouted ahead on the south fork, looking for the Great Falls the Hidatsa had told them about. He found them—a grand series of five waterfalls. The south fork was the correct route, but the expedition would have to carry everything more than 18 miles (29 km) to get around the falls!

Lewis and Clark's journey around the Great Falls was called the Great Portage.

THE WHITE CLIFFS OF THE MISSOURI

Before reaching the Great Falls, the expedition passed the White Cliffs of the Missouri. These remarkable sandstone formations seemed to the men to resemble the ruins of an ancient city. Lewis wrote that the cliffs *"with the help of a little immagination . . . are made to represent eligant [elegant] ranges of lofty freestone buildings, having their* **parapets** *well stocked with statuary . . . it seemed as if those seens [scenes] of visionary inchantment [enchantment] would never have and [an] end."*

17

CROSSING
the Great Divide

Clark described the welcome he received from Cameahwait (kam-ee-AH-wayt) and his impression of the chief: *"the Main Chief imediately tied to my hair Six Small pieces of Shells resembling perl [pearl] which is highly Valued by those people as is pr[o]cured from the nations resideing near the Sea Coast. The Great Chief . . . is a man of Influence Sence [sense] & easey & reserved manners, appears to possess a great deel of Cincerity [sincerity]."*

The expedition crossed present-day Montana and entered the Rocky Mountains—the Great Divide that separates rivers that flow east and rivers that flow west. On August 12, Lewis climbed a ridge and looked west, expecting to see a vast plain reaching toward the Pacific Ocean. Instead, he saw *"immence ranges of high mountains still to the West of us with their tops partially covered with snow."* He knew the expedition couldn't continue without horses.

This painting shows the meeting of the Corps of Discovery and the Shoshone.

On August 17, they reached a Shoshone village. To everyone's surprise, the chief was Sacagawea's brother, Cameahwait. The expedition camped nearby, learning about the land ahead from the Shoshone and preparing for the next stage of the journey. At the end of August, they set out with horses and a Shoshone guide named Old Toby.

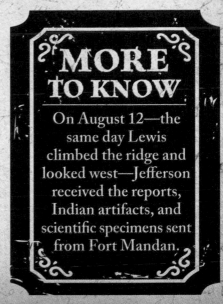

MORE TO KNOW

On August 12—the same day Lewis climbed the ridge and looked west—Jefferson received the reports, Indian artifacts, and scientific specimens sent from Fort Mandan.

On September 11, the expedition began climbing the Rockies' Bitterroot Mountains. Weather was bad, and the mountains were steep. Fallen trees made climbing even more difficult. After 3 days, Clark wrote,

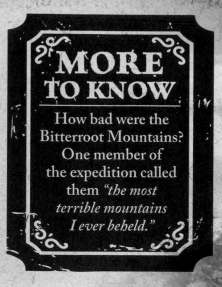

MORE TO KNOW

How bad were the Bitterroot Mountains? One member of the expedition called them *"the most terrible mountains I ever beheld."*

*"9 miles over a high mountain steep & almost inaxcessible [**inaccessible**] much falling timber which fatigues our men & horses exceedingly, in stepping over so great a number of logs added to the steep assents [ascents] and decents [descents] of the mountains . . . rained and snowed & hailed the greater part of the day all wet and cold."*

Sick and short of food, they were forced to kill and eat some of their horses. Finally, at the end of September, the starving explorers staggered out of the mountains and found themselves among the Nez Percé Indians.

With their rocky canyons, the Bitterroots are among the most impassable American peaks. The range has been called "Montana's Alps."

A CLOSE CALL

According to Nez Percé stories that have been passed down, the expedition wasn't well received at first. Some wanted to kill the strangers who had shown up unexpectedly. However, an old woman of the tribe prevented it. She had once been kidnapped by another tribe and taken to Canada. There, white people helped her escape. She returned the kindness by keeping the Nez Percé from killing the explorers.

21

From the
ROCKIES
to the Pacific

The rest of the journey would be by river, so the expedition needed to build canoes. However, their difficult mountain crossing left them too sick and weak to do anything. The day after they left the Bitterroots, Clark wrote, *"Capt. Lewis & 2 men Verry Sick this evening, my hip Verry Painfull."* He recorded similar problems the next day: *"Capt. Lewis scercely [scarcely] able to ride on a jentle horse which was furnished by the Chief, Several men So unwell that they were Compelled to lie on the Side of the road for Some time."*

OH, MY ACHING STOMACH!

The expedition's diet of dried fish and roots caused severe **indigestion**. Clark recorded days of complaints from everyone: *"men complaing [complaining] of their diat [diet] of fish & roots . . . We have nothing to eate but roots, which give the men violent pains in their bowels after eating much of them . . . I am verry sick all night, Pane [pain] in Stomach & the bowels oweing to my diet."*

Finally, some men were well enough to begin work on the canoes. On October 7, the expedition put five new canoes into the Clearwater River near present-day Orofino, Idaho, and headed west.

MORE TO KNOW

The expedition received tips on building canoes from a chief named Twisted Hair. He showed them how to use fire to hollow out pine trees.

The expedition spent about 2 1/2 weeks making canoes before starting down the Clearwater River, shown here.

Carried by the current, the expedition made swift progress down the Clearwater River, then the Snake River, and finally the Columbia River. There were many **rapids** in the rivers, however, and supplies were lost when canoes overturned or sank.

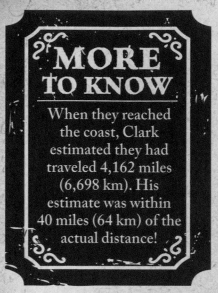

Fortunately, they were able to obtain food from Native American villages along the way.

Excitement rippled through the expedition on November 7. They thought they glimpsed the Pacific Ocean. Clark wrote, *"Great joy in camp we are in viuew [view] of the Ocian [ocean], this great Pacific Octean [Ocean] which we been so long anxious to See."* They were wrong, though. What they saw was a bay. The Pacific was still 20 miles (32 km) away. Bad weather kept them from reaching the coast for another 3 weeks.

"WET AND DISAGREEABLE"

Heavy November rains kept the expedition from moving for days at a time. The phrase *"we are all wet and disagreeable"* appears over and over in Clark's notes. As the expedition camped along the Columbia River on November 11, Clark repeated his complaint with more detail: *"most tremendious [tremendous] waves brakeing [breaking] with great violence against the Shores, rain falling in torrents, we are all wet as usual—and our Situation is truly a disagreeable one."*

Lewis and Clark and the rest of the Corps are shown at the mouth of the Columbia River.

WINTER
at Fort Clatsop

TROUBLESOME INSECTS

Besides the weather, the explorers complained frequently about fleas. In one entry, Clark griped, *"I had not been long on my mats before I was attacked most Violently by the flees and they kept up a close Siege dureing the night."* Lewis griped, *"we are infested with swarms of flees already in our new habitations; the presumption is therefore strong that we shall not devest [divest] ourselves of this intolerably troublesome vermin during our residence here."*

The expedition reached the coast in late November 1805. After exploring the area, they chose a spot on the south side of the Columbia River—near the present-day city of Astoria, Oregon—to build their winter fort. They named it Fort Clatsop after a nearby Native American tribe.

Journal entries reflect the misery caused by the weather. Clark often grumbled about rain, wind, and hail. But he felt December 30, the day they finished the fort, was a nice day: *"this day proved to be the fairest and best which we have had since our arrival at thjis [this] place, only three Showers dureing this whole day."*

Finally, in late March 1806, the expedition began the long journey home. Before leaving, they gave Fort Clatsop to the neighboring Clatsop Indians.

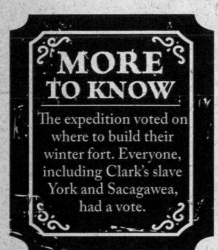

MORE TO KNOW

The expedition voted on where to build their winter fort. Everyone, including Clark's slave York and Sacagawea, had a vote.

Fort Clatsop has been rebuilt, and you can visit it to see what life was like for the expedition during the winter of 1805–1806.

FORT CLATSOP 1805-06 WINTER QUARTERS OF LEWIS AND CLARK EXPEDITION

The JOURNEY
Home

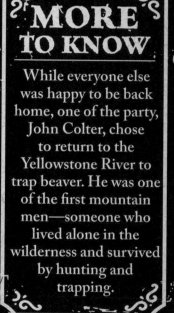

MORE TO KNOW

While everyone else was happy to be back home, one of the party, John Colter, chose to return to the Yellowstone River to trap beaver. He was one of the first mountain men—someone who lived alone in the wilderness and survived by hunting and trapping.

Fort Clatsop

The explorers reached the Nez Percé in early May 1806 and picked up their horses, which the Native Americans had cared for over the winter. After the snow melted, they crossed the Bitterroots with three Nez Percé guides. They then split into two groups to explore more of the Louisiana Territory. Lewis followed the Missouri River, while Clark followed the Yellowstone River.

In mid-August, the groups rejoined near the meeting of the two rivers. After leaving Charbonneau, Sacagawea, and her baby in the

Mandan villages, the explorers traveled swiftly down the Missouri River. They reached St. Louis on September 23, 1806, and received a hero's welcome. The long journey was over, and a new territory had been opened to Americans.

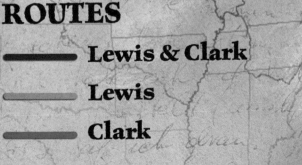

ROUTES

—— **Lewis & Clark**

—— **Lewis**

—— **Clark**

This map highlights the separate sections Lewis and Clark explored during the period they split up on their return journey.

GLOSSARY

antelope: a deerlike animal of the American West

corps: a group of people working together with a common purpose

divest: to rid

equipage: equipment

inaccessible: not reachable

indigestion: stomach discomfort or pain caused by eating something the body has trouble breaking down

malady: illness

parapet: a low wall along the edge of a roof

plains: grasslands

presumption: a belief based on the fact that something is thought to be likely

quill: a stiff, sharp, pointed hair on the body of some animals

rapid: a part of a river with a swift current and obstacles such as large rocks

tepee: a cone-shaped dwelling of some Indian tribes made of sticks and animal hides

FOR MORE
Information

Books

Perritano, John. *The Lewis and Clark Expedition*. New York, NY: Children's Press, 2010.

Pringle, Laurence. *American Slave, American Hero: York of the Lewis and Clark Expedition*. Honesdale, PA: Calkins Creek Books, 2006.

Stille, Darlene R. *The Journals of Lewis and Clark*. Chicago, IL: Heinemann Library, 2012.

Websites

Lewis & Clark
www.nationalgeographic.com/lewisandclark
Follow Lewis and Clark using an interactive journey log, read about their discoveries, find out what supplies they took, and more.

Lewis & Clark
www.pbs.org/lewisandclark
Read entries from the journals of Lewis and Clark, and delve deeply into the experiences of the Corps of Discovery.

Lewis & Clark National Historic Trail
www.nps.gov/lecl/naturescience/index.htm
Read biographies of Lewis, Clark, and others; learn about places they visited; and discover some little-known facts about the expedition.

INDEX